M000074919

to:

from:

fashion astrology

By Suzanne
Siegel Zenkel

illustrated by
diane Bigda

 Peter Pauper Press, Inc.
WHITE PLAINS, NEW YORK

for ð. m. z.,
my shining star

Illustrations copyright © 2001
Diane Bigda/Lilla Rogers Studio

Book design by Heather Zschock

Text copyright © 2001
Peter Pauper Press, Inc.
202 Mamaroneck Avenue
White Plains, NY 10601
ISBN 0-88088-842-3
Printed in China
7 6 5 4 3 2 1

Visit us at www.peterpauper.com

fashion
astrology

introduction

If you like clothes and want to feel fabulous in them, Look to the stars for inspiration. Just as your Sun sign can identify your key characteristics, it can also predict your best Look. Play up your natural strengths, feel confident, and cultivate your own great signature style—you'll quickly discover it's the one you were born with!

fashion astrology
is easier than
you think.
Let the stars—
and this book—
be your guide!

s. s. z.

aries
march 21-april 20

taurus
april 20-may 21

gemini

may 21-june 22

cancer
june 22-july 23

Leo
july 23-august 22

virgo
august 22-september 22

Libra
september 22-october 23

scorpio
october 23-november 22

sagittarius
november 22-december 22

capricorn
december 22-january 21

aquarius
january 21-february 19

pisces
february 19-march 21

aries
march 21–april 20

Let the party begin!
announces Aries, as she swaggers
in wearing low-slung metallic jeans
and an eye-poppingly tight tee shirt.
Look out for Aries! When it comes to
fashion, her motto is:
design and conquer!

aries lives on the edge, and she'd
love you to be there with her! Her pulse
quickens at the mere thought of being
first! To that end, she has invented a look
that is fashion in fast forward. But
whether she goes Disco Diva or Sassy
Schoolgirl, Aries imbues her mod style
with a touch of class.

ARIES fights for freedom of expression through her clothes. She packs a punch in whirly patterns and wild colors. She uses bright acid-toned neons to advantage, and jettisons the ones that sting. When you think "Aries style," think one big parade with oodles of popcorn, cotton candy, confetti, and fanfare!

aries' closet

a nd the most popular item in her closet would be?

Shirts—she's got rows of 'em! Solid ribbed turtlenecks (think Mary Tyler Moore) and notch-collared tunic-y blouses (think Carol Brady). Stretchy halters, one-shouldered tops, and suede-meets-wool fitted cardigans. But she's by no means stuck in the seventies! Adventurous Aries makes a fashion statement in super-chic athletic wear. Picture track-style ski pants in tech-nylon with lots of pockets. Aries can also be spotted rappelling down a snowcapped ridge in the best polar fleece she can get her hands on.

it's a wrap for aries!

A wrap *dress*, that is! This sensational staple provides day-into-night glamour. Aries goes for the finest cut, with a soft neckline and draping skirt. She keeps the look sleek by choosing monotone hose in either black or nude, or by going barelegged.

accessories

the ram's not sheepish about accessories! Aries loves pendants on long chains and straight-edged bangles—it's hip to be square! And she thinks a woolen skullcap is the perfect accent to any outfit. For insta-glam, she'll zing it up with a sequin-tile handbag, or a striped, geometric, or leopard-print scarf to tame her wild ponytail!

taurus
april 20–may 21

Some spin their wheels trying to hop the next fashion express. Taurus sits pretty, not sure what all the fuss is about! No surprise—Taurus tends to love things just the way they are. Her m.o. is to turn up the heat by fanning old fashion flames! Take one look at her oversized khakis and little-white-tee and you'll see just why those old flames never die!

taurus can make the most plain-Jane clothes sizzle! She redefines pajamas, looking almost *too* good in those drawstring bottoms and tiny tank tops.

8

taurus is grounded, dependable, calm, and loyal ... the ultimate designated driver! She's the good friend you can always count on, and her clothes are as tried and true as she is. Her beefy leather bomber jacket was probably Army Air Corps issue. Earthy Taurus is the real deal. She opts for colors from nature: alabaster, spruce, ash ...

taurus's closet

taurus uses her conservation-
ist's instinct to cultivate rare
specimens of vintage wear.
She's bullish over things that improve with age.
Snuggly cashmeres and wools (a Fair Isle
vest), slightly flared worn cords,
tight navy surplus thermals,
and play-it-again plaids
combine to form a wardrobe
that is both timeless and
super-modern. There's nothing tired about Taurus's
fatigues!

taurus's forties-inspired little black dress is the picture of elegance and sophistication.

The sleeves are short and the bodice is studded sparingly with tiny black beads. The neckline takes a V-shaped plunge and the center-slitted skirt just skims the knee. With ankle-strap high heels, the look is feminine and hip and disarmingly sexy.

accessories

Taurus Loves to go retro-
chic in accessories
that update a Look and
withstand the test of time.

She may adopt a well-made piece of
vintage jewelry (Grandma's signet
ring? Granddad's platinum watch?),

a leather-trimmed canvas messenger
bag, a jaguar-print bandanna, or
L.L. Bean Maine hunting boots . . .

Oh, and are those Meg Ryan's tiny
tinted specs she's sporting?

Gemini may 21-june 22

To watch Gemini is to watch poetry in (perpetual) motion. GEMINI THRIVES ON CHANGE, and what's easier to change than her clothes? Charming, witty, curious, alert, articulate, and eager to try anything once—GEMINI'S TALENTS ARE UNLIMITED. And so is her energy! Famous for her edgy and fresh fashion sense, Gemini loves to see herself in the best the future has to offer. If it's in the stores today, for Gemini it's probably yesterday's news!

CHEEKY GEMINI LOVES TO PLAY DRESS UP. And she always generates a buzz. She loves wisecrack colors that go SNAP, CRACKLE, AND POP! and she knows just how to adjust the volume for maximum effect. Gemini's style is strongly influenced by twin impulses which can take her from CUTE COED to VAMPY VIXEN, skipping all station stops in between!

Gemini's Closet

Gemini feels doubly blessed in . . . you guessed it, the twinset! Like Ray Ban Sunglasses, the Oreo, and the Volkswagen Beetle, sweater sets have a style that is truly flawless. Gemini views them as the quintessential answer to any fashion quandary. And they come in *so* many colors.

Gemini's a master at working the twinset to her advantage. She drapes the cardigan over her shoulders, ties it around her waist, dresses it up with fancy buttons . . . sometimes she actually even *wears* it!

"HOW COULD SOME-
THING SO GOOD BE
SO BAD?" whispers Gemini's little black

dress. Infinitely adaptable, this stunning staple

can go from zero to sixty in a nanosecond!

Homecoming Queen meet Mr. Harley-Davidson!

The dress is a long, body-grazing column with

panels of supple, lightweight leather or

Ultrasuede® in front. Boat-necked and

sleeveless—with pearls or a studded leather

collar—it's a HALLMARK OF GOOD

BREEDING OR A SIGN THAT

TROUBLE'S ON THE WAY!

Rhmmm… rhmmm!

accessories

GEMINI'S A PLAYER IN
ACCESSORIES THAT ARE
CLEVERLY OF THE
MOMENT. She teases and taunts

in feathers and fur. She blossoms in

flowers—and grows them in the

most unlikely places! She loves

gloves (all kinds), textured hosiery,

capes (and boas), kicky Lucite heels,

and techno-chic jewelry—anything

that might double her pleasure or

double her fun!

69 | CANCER

june 22-july 23

To borrow from Levi Strauss, Cancer's fashion motto is: QUALITY NEVER GOES OUT OF STYLE. The cautious crab goes out of her way to avoid fads, yet has a real handle on what looks good.

CANCER'S attachment to what's familiar translates well for her in the style department. She's a master at adapting classic chic styles to who she is now. Goodbye white cotton panties, hello French lace teddy!

69

Sensitive yet protective, Cancer may seem cool on the surface, but THE HEAT'S ON HIGH UNDERNEATH THIS CRAB'S SHELL! So high, in fact, that admirers often want to crawl in there with her.

FOR CANCER, THERE'S NOTHING VANILLA ABOUT WHITE. The very blankness of it holds its own mystique. Check how sinfully pure she looks in her tight white ribbed tank. Cancer makes a timeworn white alligator polo look like it was just designed this morning.

CANCER'S CLOSET

Lingerie has its place in Cancer's wardrobe, and that place is . . . everywhere!

She artfully uses the loveliest of undergarments to alternately disguise and reveal. Sin-sational in camisoles and bustiers, thongs and lace-top hose, push-up bras and silky slips—the mysterious beauty of what lies beneath reflects Cancer's hidden passion and warmth.

CANCER LOVES
THE CLASSIC DASH
OF THE HALTER DRESS.

In nylon and Lycra, free of frills, Cancer takes your breath away with this spine-tingling staple. She oozes demure Hollywood starlet and reveals just how sexy a shoulder can be! There's nothing more electric than the synergy of Cancer's quiet personal undertones and this dress that purrs . . .

accessories

CANCER IS JUDICIOUS IN
HER USE OF ACCESSORIES.

Taking them *off* is her way of jazzing
up an outfit! Only time-tested classics
make the cut. Think big-faced Timex
watches with oversized numbers and

bands to match. Think felt cowboy
hats and leather driving gloves and
small teardrop earrings with tiny pearls.

Think *less*. Say *more*.

Leo
juLy 23-august 22

Mirror, mirror on the wall, who's the boldest of them all? Hands down, it's Leo, who looks at her reflection, likes what she sees, and knows who she is. Her playful, flamboyant clothes warn us to make no mistake—there's nothing cowardly about *this* lion!

dramatic Leo oozes confidence. She's refreshingly up-front and fun to be around. Singularly smooth, she earns—and expects—admiration from fashion's toughest critics. Insistently provocative, Leo's style personi-fies animal magnetism at its wildest!

RED NEVER LOOKED SO HOT AS IT DOES ON LEO!

If it's good enough for a STOP sign, it's good enough for her. Leo's on fire in *anything* red, be it strapless scarlet gown or silky crimson boxer shorts. And if her flaming halter doesn't sufficiently sizzle, Leo's always got a Plan B. She's no quitter!

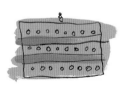

Leo's cLoset

OUCH! Leo's cLothing scorches. She generates sparks in cropped tops and sexy, slim-fitting pants. She loves shirts slinky, stretchy, puckered, gathered, sequined, or snake-skinned. She'll go bottoms up in pants with punch—studs and splashy blocks of color on cuts that ride low on the hips. But Leo never forsakes good taste in her quest for the spotlight. Her outfits are always balanced so that what's right on is never a wrong turn.

Leo's Little Black Dress isn't.

It isn't a dress, that is. She perfects master class style in a sleek menswear-inspired tuxedo pantsuit. And just how might the lion make it roar? By omitting a key component—namely, the shirt. In its place, a thin line of skin radiates heat from neck to navel. When a touch more fabric is called for, Leo's choice is a shimmery metallic shell or slouchy mesh halter. Black at its wicked best!

accessories

WHILE Leo's ultimate
accessory may well be
her self-assurance,
she's accumulated a host
of others. Glittery rhinestone

belts, satiny lace-up sandals,
fishnet hose, sequin scarves, name-

plate necklaces, studded purses, and
glaring shades of nail polish all say

look out! in a tone that's irresistible.

my VIRGO
august 22-september 22

Envision the rich luster of fine sterling silver, and you've got Virgo's look: perfectly
polished, yet full of soul. While she'll do
anything to achieve perfection, Virgo's got
a snappy city-chic look that appears to
require little, if any, maintenance. "If you
work at it hard enough, you too can look
like you *never* work at it!"

it's aLL in the details for
virgo. Her wardrobe is perfection, but
perfection is never easily won. Virgo's take
on clothing: it's all about the texture, the
cut, the trim, the color, the pattern, the
lining, the silhouette, and the quality of
the fabric (no sheen allowed).

VIRGO IS AS SHARP LOOK-
ING AS SHE IS SHARP
THINKING. Known for her clarity of
mind, she makes her mark in black and
white. She creates order out of chaos in
this classically fresh combination, which
can—and does—take her anywhere,
any time.

virgo's closet

She masterfully hones clothes of beautiful fabrics and clean lines to give them a mod-ish edge. Picture her in a tight-fit-ting black-and-white argyle short-sleeved sweater and kicky black chiffon skirt. Or walking the urban beat in a black-and-white polka-dot blouse over slim, white cigarette pants. Jackie O. sunglasses, a white turtleneck, black leather jacket, and checkered gloves bring into focus a sophistication that's sharp as a tack.

VIRGO'S A-GO-GO OVER HER LITTLE BLACK DRESS.

And you will be too! It's a sleeveless hourglass shift with a generously sized eyehole that extends from her cleavage to her neckline, and comes together in a small clasp. Worn with white gloves and fishnet hose, this sinfully simple wool crepe cocktail dress makes her the focal point at any party.

accessories

VIRGO'S ACCESSORIES
REFLECT HER
IMPECCABLE STYLE.

She takes the Barbara Bush out of
a triple strand of pearls and injects
them with a whopping dose of cool.

Other favorites may include a zebra-
print clutch, patent leather belt, wide
headband, charm bracelet, Burberry
plaid scarf, two-toned (B&W) leather
flats, and—*The New York Times.*

LIBRA

september 22–october 23

LIBRA is the consummate goodwill ambassador. She's concerned about doing the right thing and *wearing* the right thing—and it shows. Symbolized by the scales of justice, fair Libra always strives for balance and harmony.

UNITY IS AT THE CORE OF LIBRA'S WARDROBE. She keeps the peace in clothing with a cross-cultural bent. Exotic and romantic without being frou-frou, Libra has perfected her own brand of "We Are the World" chic. She weighs each element to make sure her look stays balanced and sophisticated.

Making wardrobe decisions can be tough for those who always appreciate the opposite point of view. Libra solves this problem by ᴡᴇᴀʀɪɴɢ ᴄᴏʟᴏʀꜱ ᴛʜᴀᴛ ʙʟᴇɴᴅ ᴡᴇʟʟ ᴡɪᴛʜ ᴇᴠᴇʀʏᴛʜɪɴɢ. She's very much a presence in tones that are barely there. She'll pass on colors that disturb the peace in favor of ones that work side by side. She responds to beiges, taupes, and grays for their understated elegance and universal appeal.

Libra's Closet

Compassionate Libra looks and feels her best in soft and pretty outfits. Shabby-chic fabrics mix artfully with magnificent pieces. Libra politely forgoes anything too basic in favor of filmy and flowing skirts and tops that might be exquisite imports from distant ports of call. For evening, think gossamer silk and crushed organza, shantung, and anything Far East. For weekend Libra, think gauzy peasant blouses, delicate linens, tea-stained florals, fleecy ponchos, and slim-fitting tapered pants or bell-bottom hip-huggers.

impartial Libra is partial only to little black dresses that look good from all sides.

Made of the finest silk chiffon, Libra's tantalizing feather-light dress floats in the breeze. It has sheer three-quarter length sleeves and an intricately embroidered squared-off neckline. Just below the bust is a slim satin band that ties off in the back. Libra appreciates all things beautiful, and manages like no other to elevate the little black dress to an art form.

accessories

Libra goes for accessories with a whole-earth aura that enhance her femininity. Her Turkish jewelry box holds Indian bangles, silver pieces encrusted with tiny stones, antique rings which she bands together on one finger, and chokers and wristbands of beads and fine mesh. She loves intricately beaded evening bags, no-color shimmery mules, and a special blend of essential oils that conjures up heady aromas of green tea and lemongrass.

SCORPIO
OCTOBER 23–
NOVEMBER 22

You go, girl! Intense, mysterious, and supremely powerful, Scorpio and her wardrobe say in no uncertain terms, *I'm in control*. She's got style and fashion sense to spare. Scorpio likes to wear the latest looks the hottest designers have to offer.

Scorpio's moods are changeable and so is her wardrobe. She might turn up one day in a black leather mini and the next in something soft, silken, and flowery. You might catch her at home on a rainy day in a hooded sweatshirt and a ponytail or edgy leopard pants and a little black tank—Scorpio is unpredictable!

Fiery and exciting, SCORPIO SHINES IN DEEP PURPLE. She carries off this vivid, regal color by standing tall and proud. She wears port wine to the office and burgundy to bed. Purple is sexy, pretty, and provocative, and has a shade to suit her every mood.

scorpio's closet

scorpio makes her move in clothing that works

24/7. She picks a favorite pair of black pants each season, depending on changing styles. Whatever the time, you can count on Scorpio to wear her stylish staples everywhere. Scorpio loves boots of all kinds. She doesn't consider over-the-knee boots over-the-top, and she likes to strut her stuff in cowboy boots, preferably black with fancy stitching. She'll keep wearing them—with attitude!—whether in or out of fashion.

Scorpio's Little Black Dress is a figure-hugging sheath—she likes to show off her curves!

It's sleeveless, with side-slits, and falls close to the knee. It's demure but sexy, especially with silk-satin stilettos, dangly earrings, and a string of beads. No pearls, please—much too conservative!

accessories

scorpio carries on a
special love affair
with her accessories.

They allow her to slant an outfit any
which way. She goes to extremes in
fun headgear, from baseball caps and
visors to beaded or rhinestone cocktail headbands and hair clips. She

loves to experiment with belts—
pony-skin, punched leather, chain-link—
even simple ribbons and bands.
Scorpio lets her fabulous accessories

answer her favorite question:
"Who shall I be today?"

sagittarius

november 22– december 22

Wherever sagittarius finds herself, that's where everyone wants to be. Free-spirited, optimistic, and honest, brimming with enthusiasm—she's full of spunk and spirit, and so is her wardrobe. Sagittarius is a positive thinker—and looker!

Committed to finding life's higher truths, sagittarius also finds fashion's higher hemlines Her favorite clothes change from day to day but she brings refreshing zip and flair to whatever she wears.

fit and free sagittarius is in the pink

—pink jackets, tee shirts, blouses, scarves, and, yes, pink pants and shoes, too. She loves the variety-pack aspect of pink. What other color lets you coo baby bath bubbles one day and make a dramatic entrance in fuchsia the next?

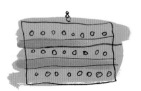

sagittarius's closet

Some items in sagittarius's closet are not up-to-the-minute—they're up-to-the-second! Her eclectic (read *electric*) wardrobe includes lots of outerwear—puffy down jackets and vests, floor-length woolens, chunky sweaters, sleek leathers, and a jeans jacket. Sagittarius collects tee shirts—all kinds—from baseball-style to baby tees with studs and rhinestones. She also loves bathing suits in groovy patterns like tie-dye and camouflage. And her collection of athletic shoes turns footwear on its heels.

sagittarius's Little Black Dress makes up in style what it Lacks in fabric.

It's strapless and simple and stops an inch above the knee. The only detailing it needs is supplied by Sagittarius's curvy shape. Fabulous as is, it can take on a multitude of looks, depending on the trimmings. Think colored or textured hose, silk shawls, strappy sandals, metallic purses, and beaded or retro-chic celluloid bangles!

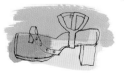

accessories

sagittarius Loves the
zing that accessories
can give an outfit, and
she wears them with
gusto! Look to Sagittarius for the
latest in colored leather goods (Let's
Go Pink) and watches banded in bril-
liant shades. She reinvents a classic
with brazenly monogrammed chunky
gold jewelry and loves wild-print cell
phone cases and bright, in-your-face
umbrellas that force everyone to
laugh at the rain.

CAPRICORN

DECEMBER 22- JANUARY 21

In clothes and in life, CAPRICORN knows what she wants and how to get it. Her style is both sophisticated and sensible, reflecting her take-charge character.

Can-do Capricorn works hard and plays hard, too. Her wardrobe, like its wearer, says "BRING IT ON—I'M READY!" She can morph effortlessly from casual chic to ultraglam, but no matter where she turns up, her fashion mantra is always, *Simplicity!*

BASIC BLACK WORKS BLACK MAGIC WHEN CAPRICORN WEARS IT!

Its richness mirrors the power that lies within—*and* it goes with everything! Capricorn looks equally smart dressed down in a sleek three-quarter length black leather jacket and dressed up in a smoldering silk slip-dress of the same color. Cool Capricorn always dresses the part of her got-it-all-together image.

capricorn's closet

capricorn is crazy for shoes!

She considers them an investment and springs
for well-made styles that last.
Capricorn goes for quality over
quantity when it comes to
footwear. Her current favorite is
a high-heeled pointy black satin
slingback. It looks drop-dead
when paired with skinny black
pants or a backless ballgown.
Straightforward Capricorn steers
clear of anything too ruffled, fringed,
or embellished.

styLe meets substance with capricorn's Little black dress:

just above the knee, but subtly suggestive in its purity of line. The neckline is sublimely elegant, revealing only enough décolletage to spur the imagination. A simple slit in the hemline may be just the right touch. Think Barbra Streisand, not Jennifer Lopez, on this one. Capricorn knows where her strengths lie, and she *never* looks like she's trying too hard.

accessories

Just a touch of sparkle is enough for Capricorn! The look is clean and neat. She's apt to arrive on time sporting a classic Cartier-inspired tank watch with a black band. Capricorn likes to go debutante-chic with a single strand of pearls, super-size tortoiseshell sunglasses, velvet headbands, fur-trimmed hats or gloves in animal prints, and hefty chain-link bracelets and belts in gold or silver. Think glamour, not glitz.

aquarius
january 21-february 19

Marching fashionably to her own drummer, aquarius gets first prize for originality! Look to her for the ultimate in creative style solutions.

Opposites often attract, and aquarius is the one most likely to show up in white lace and motorcycle boots! The components of her outfit may not always tell the same story, but the overall look is invariably a bestseller.

EVER THE IDEALIST, AQUARIUS MAY LITERALLY AND FIGURATIVELY LOOK AT THE WORLD THROUGH ROSE-COLORED LENSES! No surprise that the water bearer makes a splash in soft blushing tones. Her sunny disposition is best reflected in the warm dusty colors she combines inventively.

aquarius's cLoset

tHere's NOTHING HumOruM aBOUT aquarIus or tHe CONTENTS OF HER CLoset!

She goes for skirts that surprise, with asymmetrical hemlines. And she loves to collect fabulous sweaters; experimenting with textile and design, she treasures each one for its unique appeal. She looks equally fabulous in hooded pullovers

and coat-length cardigans. Her first choice may be an elegant, loosely crocheted, tight fitting scoop neck. Do I hear Fleetwood Mac in the background?

tнe past coLLiðes wiтн тнe pReseNт wнeN it comes to aquarius's LittLe bLack ðress.

She raids everyone's closet to find the best in vintage. Aquarius resurrects the 1920s in a soft, beaded silk-chiffon dress, sleeveless and squared at the neck, that falls almost to the ankle. The past never looked so good!

accessories

think flea market funk when you think aquarius. She's got the knack!

She loves anything that's made of lace or that laces up—from long-sleeved tees to Victorian kid ankle boots. Her jewelry box overflows with vintage belt buckles in hand-tooled silver;

simple bar-pins, enameled or with small stones; delicate antique gold rings and earrings; cameo chokers, silver cobweb necklaces, and anything marcasite.

pisces

february 19-march 21

When it comes to spotting the next sweeping fashion trend, the fish rules. Still waters run deep for perceptive Pisces. Don't be fooled by her dreamy exterior—she had you figured out at *hello!*

PISCES'S SIXTH SENSE WORKS MAGIC WHEN APPLIED TO STYLE. She may hiss at the latest snakeskin print, but you can bet she saw it coming! She expresses her spiritual side through the clothes she chooses. What a revelation to spot her in a sheer, silk-screened, flouncy blouse à la Michelle Pfeiffer. Pisces doesn't analyze her dreams—she wears them!

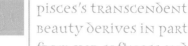

pisces's transcendent beauty derives in part from her softness and sincerity. Anything faux is a faux pas! And Pisces's clothes are as true blue as she is! She's blissful in the cool serenity of blue, from sky to midnight and every hue in between. Yes, that *was* Pisces sitting by the dock of the bay in her blue-and-white French sailor boat-neck!

pisces' closet

it's in the jeans for pisces!
when it comes to denim, she
just can't get enough—dark and
stiff, or faded and worn! Pisces gets the blue
ribbon for making jeans work for her.
She gives them a sharp downtown
edge with a steely metal belt or
pairs them with cowboy boots for
weekend comfort. But tender-hearted

Pisces wouldn't want her
torso to feel left out. She
patches things up in an over-
dyed denim jacket or shirt.
Go go indigo!

PISCES SKIRTS THE ISSUE OF THE LITTLE BLACK DRESS BY STANDING OUT IN SEPARATES. She may breeze by in a crinkled silk organza blouse and clingy crepe skirt, or an angora sweater and silk charmeuse pants. Depending on her mood, the look is elegant or easy-going. Always aware of her place and how she fits in, Pisces knows how to wear her clothes, and never lets her clothes wear her.

accessories

Pisces HAS A LOT OF BAGGAGE, BUT NOT THE KIND THAT WEARS YOU DOWN. She rejects the portable office that a tote affords in favor of stylish slouch. Backpacks and hobos in supple leathers, suedes, and unusual fabrics take her where she wants to go. Pisces is likely to dab her body with a custom-made scent suggesting the ocean and its native grasses. For jewelry, think simple silver banded rings and hoop earrings in varied sizes.